C000001256

Maximizing Your Potential

How to become the best version of yourself by taking charge, getting ahead, and knowing your strength to live a fulfilled life. (Vol. 2)

Adebayo F. Dorcas

Table of Contents

Copyright © 2022 Adebayo F. Dorcas

All rights reserved. No part of this publication may be reproduced, distributed or transmitted in any form or by any means, including photocopying, recording, or other electronic or mechanical methods without the prior written permission of the publisher, except in the case of brief quotations embodied in critical reviews and specific other non-commercial uses permitted by copyright law.

Preface

Many people believe that their abilities are restricted. In reality, you may have a skewed perception of what you're capable of accomplishing.

It is, nevertheless, possible to overcome your restrictions and reach your entire potential. The idea is to recognize that you have the ability to grow and develop. When you do, you'll be able to broaden your perception of what you're capable of and achieve more than you ever imagined.

What opportunities are you passing up because you aren't utilizing your potential? This book contains the solution to that question.

It's a book I'm looking forward to and have been waiting for. Because there is so much material in this book, digesting it all would take a lifetime. So let me tell you a little bit about the book. It's about how to maximize your potential and achieve greatness. It's about how to better yourself, how to become more productive, and how to get your life back on track. The book begins with a basic premise: we are all born with the same amount of energy and ability, but we all use it in various ways. Some individuals utilize their energy to accomplish a lot, while others use it to procrastinate. You get to choose which one you want to be.

Introduction

"We are all born with the same amount of energy and ability, but we all use it in various ways".

You're wasting your time if you're not making the most of your ability. Knowing your abilities isn't enough; you also need to put them to good use.

It's time to focus on the "how" rather than the "what" if you want to get the most out of your life. What actions must you take to achieve the pinnacle of your profession? What tactics can you employ to maximize your assets? Are you certain that you have what it takes to reach your greatest potential? This book will show you how to achieve all of your objectives while being stress-free.

You must first acknowledge your strengths in order to make the most of them. This course will show you how to do just that. We'll look at how to discover your strengths and then put that information to work for you. Consider how you can apply your unique skills in your professional and personal life once you've identified them:

- What tasks do you think you'd be better at than other people?

- How can you take advantage of your unique abilities to boost your career?

- How can you improve your quality of life by utilizing your unique abilities?

The answers to these questions may be found all over this book and will help you decide which route to choose.

This book will show you how to take some of the required measures to reach your full potential in life. You're wasting your time if you're not making the most of your ability. Knowing your abilities isn't enough; you also need to put them to good use. It's time to focus on the "how" rather than the "what" if you want to get the most out of your life. What actions must you take to achieve the pinnacle of your profession? What tactics can you employ to maximize your assets? Are you certain that you have what it takes to reach your greatest potential? This book will show you how to achieve all of your objectives while being stress-free. You must first acknowledge your strengths in order to make the most of them. This course will show you how to do just that. We'll look at how to discover your strengths and then put that information to work for you. Once you've identified your unique qualities, think about how you can put them to use in your job and personal life. What tasks do you think you'd be better at than other people? How can you take advantage of your unique abilities to boost your career? How can you improve your quality of life by utilizing your unique abilities? The answers to these questions will help you make a choice. This course will

11

cover the following subjects: What are their advantages? What methods do you use to identify your own particular strengths? What's the difference between an individual's assets and liabilities? What criteria do you use to assess your own abilities? What can you do to maximize the value of your assets? How do you go about achieving your objectives? What are some ideas for making the most of your abilities? How do you intend to attain your objectives? Is it possible for you to provide me with any tips on how to live a happy life? What do you think is the most pleasurable way to live? What's the most efficient way to achieve success?

Chapter 1

The Human Potential Maximizers

The human potential maximizer is someone who seizes chances and maximizes their potential. It's not so much about what you can do as it is about how much value you add to others. It doesn't matter if you make the most of yourself if you don't have an impact on your life. People that have a good effect on their lives are needed in the world. There isn't such a thing as a failed individual.

There are several strategies to increase productivity, including: Make a priority list for yourself. Determine your essential values and then behave in accordance with them. Concentrate on one item at a time and give it your all. If you want to become more productive, you must first establish your priorities. You must ensure that your time is used in a manner that is consistent with your ideals. What are your core beliefs? What are your guiding principles? You must ensure that your actions are consistent with your basic principles. If it isn't, you will most likely become bored and go on to something else. The strength of values is that it gives you a feeling of purpose in life when you connect your activities with your ideals. Your values will guide your life and provide you with the motivation to achieve your goals. Make a priority list for yourself. It is not necessary to have a master plan. Simply establish a list of your top objectives and get to work. What are your main concerns? What are you working on at the moment? When do you expect to be finished? What do you want to achieve? How long do you believe it will take? This is an excellent place to begin. It might assist you in identifying the areas where you should concentrate your efforts.

Many professionals are finding that maximizing the potential of others is a skill that they need to use more and more in their everyday lives. It's one of the most underappreciated yet crucial abilities, and if used correctly, it may help you boost your team's overall productivity and performance. This section offers suggestions for maximizing your employees' human potential by enhancing their motivation, drive, and creativity in a way that makes them feel good about what they're doing.

-Motivation: Motivating your team is the first step in maximizing their human potential. A stimulus elicits an emotional reaction, which is referred to as motivation. It's why we become thrilled about new or interesting things, or why we're motivated to finish a task. Motivation originates from the inside, but it may also be induced from the outside. If you want to increase your team's productivity, motivation, and creativity, you should concentrate on how to increase internal motivation. The most common method for boosting motivation is to

- To provide individuals with what they desire or need in order to complete their tasks. Reward and recognition systems are based on this premise.

- Incentives can also be used to inspire individuals. If you're teaching your staff to be more productive, you may give them a bonus for finishing a project ahead of schedule, or even a bonus for reaching a set level of productivity.

- Allowing individuals to express themselves is another method to boost motivation. It's critical to provide a comfortable environment in which individuals may be creative, express themselves, and have fun. People who believe they are in an atmosphere where they can be creative, think freely, and express themselves are more likely to be motivated, and hence perform better.

- Finally, the most efficient way to boost motivation is to understand your team's needs and wants. If you do it well, you'll be able to tap into their desire and drive, resulting in increased productivity and enhanced performance. You may take actions to enhance people's motivation after you understand how they operate and what inspires them.

-Improve your people's drive and creativity: The next stage in optimizing your team's human potential is to improve your people's drive and creativity. Because they don't understand their team members' demands, many professionals struggle to motivate their teams. You must tap into your team's desire and imagination if you want them to be more productive, motivated, and innovative. To boost people's motivation and inventiveness,

- You must first comprehend their desires and motivations. Telling folks what you want them to do isn't enough. You must also comprehend their motivations.

- Determine what motivates your employees. This is critical since you want to concentrate on the things that inspire them. Do they like assisting others? Are they motivated by monetary gain? Are they driven by a desire to be recognized? People might be motivated by a variety of other things. You must discover what motivates your team in order to motivate them appropriately.

- Helping people conquer their worries is another way to boost their motivation and inventiveness. Many professionals are afraid of failure, public speaking, and simply speaking with new people.When you can assist others in overcoming their worries, they become more motivated and inventive. This is due to their willingness to take chances and attempt new things.

- Also, think about what you can do to help them. As a leader, it's critical that you assist your team members in seeing what they can do to advance their careers. This may be accomplished in a variety of ways, but one of the most successful is by assisting them in comprehending their influence. This is when the approach of "I'm the reason you're here" comes into play. This can be accomplished in a variety of ways.

When it comes to human potential, the biggest error entrepreneurs make is failing to recognize what we already have. This encompasses a wide range of talents, including our physical, mental, emotional, and spiritual capacities. Instead of relying on the same old, tired assumptions about what we are capable of, the goal is to tap into these abilities and exploit them to their maximum potential. You can make the most of your skills and be more productive than you ever imagined once you learn to recognize the resources that already exist inside you.

Many individuals have told me that they are too preoccupied to work on themselves, but the truth is that you can't get anywhere without first working on yourself. This isn't always simple, but it's one of the most crucial things you can do. You should schedule time for personal development since it will help you be more productive at work and feel better in general. Here are some of the places where you should concentrate your efforts:

1. Physical Health: Because I am not a physician, I am unable to provide medical advice. However, it appears to me that many individuals are unaware of the necessity of excellent physical health. Our bodies play a vital role in our lives. We can't accomplish anything without it. It's also a complicated situation. The human body has its own mechanism for maintaining health and function.

2. Mental Health: I'm not a psychologist, but it appears to me that many individuals are unaware of the significance of mental health. Many people suffering from mental illness wait a long time to seek treatment.

3. Financial Health: I'm not a financial counselor, but it appears to me that many individuals underestimate the value of financial health. It's not only about going into debt; it's also about how you deal with it. You will have more freedom in life if you have a solid financial status. It will also keep you from turning into a statistic. When I first got married, we had a lot of credit cards.

4. Spiritual Health: I am not a religious leader, but I believe that many people are unaware of the significance of spiritual health.

There are a variety of strategies to improve your spiritual health, and many of them necessitate a relationship with your creator. For some, a religious group, such as a church, may be the answer. Others may find this through a non-religious group such as a book club or a group of pals.

5. *Social Health:* I'm not a social worker, but it appears to me that many individuals are unaware of the significance of social health. The state of mind in which we are able to sustain the social interactions that are necessary for our survival and enjoyment is referred to as "social health." Social health is the consequence of a continuous process of forming and maintaining supportive and meaningful interpersonal interactions.

6. *Political Health*: I am not a politician, but it appears to me that many people are unaware of the significance of political health. I believe it is critical for us to recognize that we are participants in a political system. We play a role in the political system. It is critical that we recognize the importance of maintaining our political health.

7. *Environmental Health:* Although I am not an environmental scientist, I believe that many individuals are unaware of the relevance of environmental health. This is especially true, in my opinion, for young people who are unaware of their environmental influence. There are various facets to this that must be comprehended. One is that we must make better use of our resources.

8. *Cultural Health:* I am not a cultural historian, but I believe that many people are unaware of the significance of cultural health. I believe I can speak for everyone in the field when I say we're all ill. We have come to embrace the notion that we are all victims of our cultures and that, in order to be healthy, we must transform our cultures. It's good if you're a realist with few options, but I believe there's a lot of potential for a movement that embraces the concept of a society as a culture.

The Human Potential Maximizers That Are Most Underutilized

Human potential is the capacity to apply one's knowledge, talents, and experiences to obtain more happiness, joy, and fulfillment. Human potential is a method of thinking about people's ability to develop and evolve. People change and evolve all the time, yet the changes might be subtle or noticeable. Understanding human potential and how to build and develop it in ourselves, our children, and our students is critical.

There are certain human potential maximizers that are far too underutilized in today's environment. You're probably squandering your time, energy, and resources if you're not using them. It's also time to start utilizing them if you haven't already. They are known as "Human Potential Maximizers" because they assist us in reaching our full potential.

Human potential maximizers are one of the most underutilized personal development instruments available today. Although we all have the same potential, some people are better at realizing it than others. Some people aren't particularly excellent at anything, while others excel in all areas. It all depends on how they use what they've got. Certain people are above average in some areas and below average in others. In contemporary culture, there are certain human potential maximizers that aren't employed nearly enough.

They are a group of individuals who are unique in some manner. These potential maximizers are some of the most popular people utilized as role models when talking about personal growth and life improvement. They are the folks who have brilliant ideas and can put them into practice. They are individuals that excel in one area while falling short in others. They're the ones who can excel at one thing while failing miserably at another. Some of these

25

individuals are well-known, while others are not. The following is a list of prospective maximizers:

- o **The High Achiever:** A high achiever is sometimes confused with an overachiever, although the two are not synonymous. A high achiever is someone who has a lot of different things going for them and is able to make great use of what they have. An overachiever is someone who is extremely good at one thing, whereas an overachiever is someone who is very good at one thing.

- o **The Perfectionist:** A perfectionist is someone who is always looking for ways to better themselves. They strive for perfection in all they do, and this is what propels them forward.

- o **A Great Leader:** A great leader is someone who can lead a group of people to achieve something amazing while inspiring others in the process.

- **A Creative Thinker:** is someone who can come up with a variety of approaches to accomplish the same goal. They are highly creative and have the ability to think beyond the box.

- **The Outspoken One:** An outspoken person is someone who is not afraid to speak their mind and is likely to share their thoughts and ideas with others.They are frequently open and honest, and they have a tendency to speak their views.

- **A Loyal Friend:** is someone who will always stand by your side, even if you aren't perfect. They will not pass judgment on you, but will instead stand by your side in all you do.

- **The Risk Taker**: Someone who is willing to take chances in life is known as a risk-taker. They aren't scared to take risks or attempt new things. They are entertaining to be around because they have a sense of adventure.

- o **The Dreamer:** Someone who has the ability to imagine huge dreams is known as a dreamer. They're always on the lookout for the next great thing, and they're prepared to go to any length to make their fantasies come true.

- o **The Optimist:** An optimist is someone who always sees the bright side of things and can assess a situation from all angles. They see the best in everyone and everything, which allows them to achieve great things.

Human potential maximizers are a notion that has existed since the beginning of time. However, it's just recently gotten a lot of attention and is a fantastic method to create leads and boost revenue. Human potential maximizers have been demonstrated time and time again. People who are dedicated to bettering themselves earn more money than those who are not. They are more likely to be successful in their careers and to be happier.

What Is the Importance of Human Potential Maximization? Maximizers are more likely to be happy, successful, and healthy. Because it helps you sell more of your products or services, human potential optimization is a great marketing strategy. It also assists you in identifying those who are likely to purchase from you. Maximizers are the best employees because they are laser-focused on their goals. They are also among the most well-liked individuals in any area. They have a higher chance of becoming successful in their jobs and are generally happier. Maximizing human potential has been shown time and time again.

The only way to reach your full potential is to work on yourself. Each of us has our own set of limitations. We will automatically discover and progress past those boundaries if we push ourselves to achieve more and attempt new things. It's the only way to advance.

What does it take to unleash your full potential as a human being?

The answer to that question isn't always evident, but acknowledging that you can is the first step. You have the capacity to do anything once you stop restricting yourself, and there are no boundaries to what you can do. You are more than the sum of your accomplishments. You have the ability to change your life and your destiny. You may be joyful and successful at the same time. You have the potential to do great things.

In today's corporate world, we can't avoid dealing with change. We will stagnate and fail if we do not accept the changes and challenges that surround us. There are actions we can take to help us remain adaptable, resilient, and flexible in the face of shifting circumstances and obstacles. No matter what sort of business you're in, we'll discuss four tools that can help you reach your maximum potential.

- **Learning to "Watch" People and Circumstances:** Learning to observe people and situations is one of the most essential things you can do to reach your maximum potential. Through observation, we may learn about what is going on around us. We may learn from other people's motivations. We can learn how they act and why they act in certain ways. We can figure out what their advantages and disadvantages are. By observing them, we can learn how they think. Learning how others act may teach us a lot about ourselves. According to an old adage, it's not what you know, it's who you know. It's vital that you grasp this notion if you want to be successful. It's not only about being able to pick up fresh information; it's about being able to observe people and circumstances as well. You'll be able to see the chances and challenges that are available to you when you accomplish this. You'll be able to spot when others are acting productively or destructively, and you'll be able to capitalize on these possibilities and problems. It's critical to understand how to think in reverse, learn in reverse, and observe in reverse. You'll be able to reach your full potential after you understand how to perform these things. We are prone to being locked in our routines. We might grow so accustomed to doing things the same way every day that we lose sight of the reality that there are alternative possibilities.

o **Set Objectives:** What are you attempting to achieve? Do you wish you had more time to spend with your loved ones? Do you have a specific financial objective in mind? Do you want to improve your physical condition?It's critical that you set goals for everything you wish to do. What's the sense of accomplishing anything if you don't have any goals? And if you don't have objectives, you won't be able to tell if you're on course to meet them or not. When we set goals, we may focus our attention on one subject at a time. We have the ability to set ourselves up for success. We can ensure that we are taking constructive action toward our objectives every day, and we can keep ourselves motivated by ensuring that we are succeeding. You'll be able to do a lot more if you have a strategy in place than if you're simply winging it. It's easy to become engrossed in the now and lose sight of our objectives. We'll be able to stay focused on what we want if we keep our eyes on the goal.

o **Make a Future Vision:** What do you want your life to be like in the future? If you want to do something significant in your life, you must first create a vision for the future. This vision will assist you in remaining focused. It will assist you in remaining motivated. It will assist you in remaining disciplined. It will assist you in avoiding distractions and remaining focused on your objectives. However, if you don't have a future vision, you'll wind up doing things that won't get you where you want to go. You won't have any sense of direction or concentration in your life.

o **Create a Successful Environment:** When you create a successful atmosphere, you're ensuring that you're doing all possible to ensure your success. By obtaining the appropriate tools, adopting the correct mentality, and taking the right steps, you're putting yourself in a position to succeed. You'll find yourself in a scenario where you don't feel successful if you don't accomplish these things.

When people feel as though they don't have anything to do or can't accomplish anything, they might quickly become disheartened. No matter how hard you try or how hard you work, if you don't believe in yourself, you will never be able to achieve your goals. Even if you don't believe it, you should always be able to achieve more and do better. You can do more than you think, whether you are a man or a woman. Everyone has the ability to achieve their goals. You are the same as everyone else. Start doing anything. That's all you need to do. The first step is to get started, and the second is to go a step further. This will assist you in learning new things, honing your talents, and boosting your self-assurance. No one else will believe in you if you don't believe in yourself.

Finally, as people begin to realize their full potential, they begin to grow. The first step is for them to think that they can make a difference. The next stage is to concentrate on the correct things and improve at them. The next phase is to keep strengthening your sense of self. When the first two are completed, the third is generally completed in less than a year. I share this with you because I want you to understand that altering your habits and repetitious behavior is the key to being a better, more productive, and better person. This, I feel, is the fundamental key to having a better life.

If you're ready to start making positive changes in your life, I've got some wonderful news for you. You can finish it in a single day! What you must do is begin right now. Don't put it off till tomorrow or next week. Begin today and never look back.

***Summary:** If you want to become more productive, you must first establish your priorities. Determine your essential values and then behave in accordance with them. Focus on one item at a time and give it your all.*

Motivation originates from the inside, but it may also be induced from the outside.

The most efficient way to boost motivation is to understand your team's needs and wants. This will enable you to tap into their desire and drive for increased productivity and enhanced performance. As a leader, it's critical that you assist your team members in seeing what they can do to advance their careers. Many professionals are afraid of failure, public speaking, and speaking with new people. Helping people conquer their worries is another way to boost their motivation and inventiveness.

Many people are unaware of the importance of financial and spiritual health. Financial Health is about going into debt and how you deal with it. Social Health is the consequence of forming and maintaining meaningful interpersonal interactions.

Human potential is the capacity to apply one's knowledge, talents, and experiences to obtain more happiness, joy, and fulfillment.

There are certain human potential maximizers that are far too underutilized in today's environment. It's time to start utilizing them if you haven't already. An overachiever is someone who is extremely good at one thing. A perfectionist is always looking for ways to better themselves. Someone who is willing to take chances in life is known as a risk-taker.

Maximizing human potential has been shown time and time again. Maximizers are the best employees because they are laser-focused on their goals. They are also among the most well-liked individuals in any area

It's critical to understand how to think in reverse, learn in reverse and observe in reverse. You'll be able to see the chances and challenges that are available to you when you do this. We are prone to being locked in our routines because we lose sight of alternatives. If you don't have a future vision, you'll end up doing things that won't get you where you want to go. You can do more than you think, whether you are a man or a woman. Everyone has the ability to achieve their goals.

Chapter 2

The Psychology of Human Potential

The human mind is both complicated and strong. You build your distinct personality and come to understand yourself better as you grow from infancy to maturity and beyond, but we typically feel constrained in some manner. Because of our perceived limits, we frequently hold ourselves back, which prevents us from becoming our best selves.

People have the ability to develop into amazing human beings at any age, from childhood to old age. What if you could use psychology to tap into this latent potential and live your greatest life? When we think of a hero, we think of someone who has overcome adversity and transformed it into a source of strength in their lives. Their success is what defines them. What happens, though, if you lose?

How many times have you heard someone say that everything has its time and place? While this principle holds true in other aspects of life, it does not apply to business success.

Understanding the psychology of human potential is the best approach to getting there, whether you're in school, running a business, or trying to become a better version of yourself. We're not talking about how much weight you can lift or how quickly you can run; we're talking about your mindset. When you research human behavior, you will discover that various psychological elements impact people's decisions and actions.

When we talk about human potential, we generally refer to potential that is greater than what we have previously accomplished. We're talking about the possibility that everyone of us has to grow into our full potential. We know this because we watch people evolve and grow in a variety of ways throughout their lives. Some people progress to the point that they are better versions of themselves than they were previously, while others remain unchanged or even regress. However, I think that everyone of us has the potential to be even better than we are today, and that this potential may be realized by taking steps toward personal improvement.

It is a prevalent misconception that in order to obtain more out of life, we must modify our conduct. However, as we'll learn in this book, human potential is determined by our mentality rather than our deeds. In order to achieve our goals, we frequently need to adjust our conduct, which is a component of the physical environment. Most individuals, on the other hand, feel that in order to be happy, they must make changes in their lives. This book illustrates how the reverse is true: we must change our thinking in order to attain our objectives. Our ideas have such power that they may work miracles. We can use our minds to solve all of our issues and accomplish all of our objectives. Knowing how to focus our thoughts is the key to success.

I think that we can all achieve greatness. I believe that everyone can succeed, that we are not restricted by society's expectations, that we are defined more by what we do than what we own, and that if you keep taking action and thinking positively, you can achieve anywhere you want to go.

The psychology of life and business optimization is distinct from other forms of psychology. It's not simply about getting more out of life. Getting the most out of life and achieving the maximum level of enjoyment is what optimizing life entails. Discovering what we need in life and then using it to achieve what we want to do is what optimizing life is all about. It's not about living on the edge or being terrified of happiness. It's all about choosing decisions that will lead to a life of plenty, joy, and serenity. It's easy to see how we can make our lives better. Every day, we have the ability to make better decisions.

How can I do more with less effort?

When did you last feel like you were "doing too much"? I'm sure it wasn't just a few days ago. Even if you're working really hard right now, you're undoubtedly aware that your burden is increasing. Working harder and longer isn't the answer for many individuals. In reality, it is frequently ineffective. According to studies, the average worker loses three hours each week owing to stress and other variables associated with overworking. Here are six practices that can help you get more done with less effort to keep your productivity high while limiting the quantity of labor you do:

- **Focus on the Important Stuff:** Deciding what's important and what's not is the first step toward getting more done. The simplest method to achieve this is to make a list of everything you need to get done and rank them in order of importance. This is a basic yet efficient technique for staying focused on the most critical activities. If your to-do list is getting out of hand, it's time to take a step back and figure out what really has to be done right now.

- **Set Realistic Objectives:** Setting realistic goals is one of the most effective techniques to ensure your success. An aim is a desire for something to happen in the future. Setting too ambitious objectives can frequently lead to disappointment. On the other hand, setting excessively modest ambitions might lead to failure. Make sure your goals are reasonable to avoid these problems. For example, if you want to lose weight, don't set a target of losing 10 pounds in one week. Instead, establish a weekly weight loss target of one pound. This will help you stay focused on your objective and lower your chances of giving up before you achieve it.

- **Divide labor into tasks by breaking it down.** Breaking down a task into smaller parts should be done before you begin. This aids in staying organized and keeping track of your progress. It also makes the process easier to accomplish because you won't be sidetracked by little things. If you're working on one, you could wish to break down each aspect of a project into smaller, more manageable jobs. This will allow you to concentrate on only one aspect at a time, preventing you from being overwhelmed.

- **Make a list of your priorities.** This will assist you in completing more tasks. You'll have to make some difficult choices in this situation. For example, which of your tasks do you think is the most important? Should you devote more time to the most critical tasks and less time to the less important ones? When there are too many things to do, it's easy to become overwhelmed, but it's also critical not to put off any job that has to be done. The best way to accomplish this is to concentrate on the top three tasks that you know must be completed. Move on to the following three things on your list once you've done them.

- **Take Breaks:** It's important to take breaks even if you're working long hours and doing a lot of things. Burnout, a mental and physical condition of tiredness and fatigue that can develop when you're always working hard, can be caused by staying concentrated for too long. Take a few minutes to relax instead of focusing on what you have to do by going for a stroll outside or eating a snack. If you're feeling overwhelmed, delegate a tiny portion of your tasks to someone else. Don't just sit there idling your time away!

- **Get the Correct Equipment:** If you want to get more done, make sure you have the right tools for the job. Some chores are made simpler when you use a specialized tool. For example, if you're creating a website, you may require certain software. If you are unsure, ask someone who knows what software you require. They'll be able to provide you with advice based on their own experiences. Also, if you're doing something you've never done before, be sure you have all of the supplies and tools you'll need to complete the project. This way, you won't have to waste time looking for them.

Everyone carries a unique gift inside them. Even if you haven't found your calling yet, you should never give up. Working on your potential and giving it your all is the best way to discover your talent. Your potential is made up of a mix of natural abilities and learned skills.

It is critical to cultivate your skills since they are one of the most significant factors in achieving success. People should always strive to improve their skills since they are capable of far more than they currently do. Finding your talent is the most important thing. You must not squander your time on insignificant matters.

When it comes to honing your skills, it's important to keep a positive mindset. You'll never succeed at this if you don't feel you have the ability. You must utilize your intellect. You must realize that it is feasible to improve your abilities. This is a critical point. Don't put off honing your skills. You must act immediately.

You should perform the following if you wish to increase your abilities:

*Concentrate on your objectives.

*Put forth your best effort.

*Set the proper objectives.

*Do not accept "no" as a response.

Many people believe that the most difficult component of any profession is the first step. However, this is not the case; the next stages are the most difficult. If you want to improve your skills, you must work hard and focus on your objectives. You should make every effort to realize your full potential and never give up. Many people lack the guts to pursue their passions, but this does not imply that they are failures. All you have to do now is summon the confidence to pursue your passions. You will become a better person as a result of this.

The Psychology of Life and Business

Optimization

Someone once stated, "Optimism is a tremendous asset." This is especially true in the corporate sector, where how you manage your resources may make the difference between success and failure. As a consequence, learning how to nurture optimism and keep a positive mindset is critical for anybody running a business. The truth is that optimism has become ingrained in our daily lives.

You can't rely on your intuition or gut feelings alone when it comes to optimizing for outcomes, and you shouldn't expect to succeed without putting in the effort. It's critical to realize that the world's most successful individuals don't suddenly decide to do what they do best one day; they've been working toward that objective for a long time. You are in the same boat.

When it comes to your life and career, optimization means doing the things you should be doing to move ahead—but haven't been doing because of the plethora of distractions and unnecessary chores that constantly seem to consume more time than you desire.

There has been a significant shift in the way individuals approach life and work in today's corporate climate. It's a move away from "living and working" and toward "optimizing their lives and business." If you're not making a conscious effort to do so, you're likely missing out on a fantastic opportunity. We may be quite short-sighted when it comes to improving our lives and enterprises, with our gaze concentrated on a single objective or project. You may do so much more than you ever imagined possible by taking a step back and taking the time to improve your life and company. I'm sure you understand what I'm talking about. You're working on a project and can't see the forest for the trees since you're so engrossed in it. Your priorities are all over the place, and maintaining a sense of balance is nearly impossible. You may work 60 hours a week, but your family suffers as a result of your insufficient time with them. Perhaps you're simply too busy to spend meaningful time with your spouse or children. It may appear that having it all is impossible. But here's the thing: if you want to be truly successful in your life and career, you must learn to maximize both.

Stop doing things in the short term if you want to optimize your life and business. This entails planning ahead of time what you're going to do and how you'll get there. When you plan forward, you build a sense of excitement and anticipation for what is ahead. You'll begin to feel more enthusiastic about the tasks you're working on, making it simpler to stay focused on your long-term objectives. But, if you're like most people, getting past your immediate requirements to ensure that you're making the best judgments isn't always simple. You don't have time to pause and consider what you'll be doing in the future. Instead, you get caught up in the moment and do whatever seems to be the simplest thing at the time, which frequently results in a lot of wasted time and energy. As a result, you may find it more difficult to achieve your long-term objectives than if you had taken the time to optimize your life and business. The notion of "living and working" becomes extremely significant at this point. Living and working is a mentality that focuses on long-term objectives rather than present necessities. You start to get more done when you are completely focused on what is in front of you. This is why you must stop living in the now and begin living and working in the future. For most individuals, this is a new way of thinking since they spend the majority of their time and energy worrying about what will happen next rather than living and working. You must, however, make this shift if you are serious about maximizing your life and business. Because you'll be shocked at how much time you'll save and how much more progress you'll make once you do. This is also why you must be deliberate with your time; you do not have time to be distracted by immediate requirements. Instead, you should concentrate on your long-term objectives and the activities necessary to attain them. This will assist you in staying on track and ensure that you are progressing toward your objectives rather than drifting aside.

Business owners are continuously seeking methods to develop and improve their companies. They are continuously seeking the greatest strategy to ensure that their lives and enterprises are optimized. If you're a businessperson, you're well aware that everything you do has an influence on your company. As a result, when it comes to your business, you must have a goal. The reason you do what you do is because you have a goal. Your business revolves around your aim.

If you're in sales, you want to optimize your sales. If you're in management, you want to optimize your earnings. If you work in marketing, you want to get as much exposure as possible. If you work in advertising, you want to get the most bang for your buck. If you work in manufacturing, you want to get the most out of your time. If you work in finance, you probably want to make the most money possible.

10 Steps to Realizing Your Full Potential

Consider the events that have occurred in your life and how you feel about each one. There's a lot of space for improvement and growth here. You can't afford to repeat your mistakes from the previous year. I'd advise you to find a method to reconnect with the positive aspects of life and the accomplishments you've already made.

This will give you a better understanding of where you are today and how to use it to help you develop and improve. Consider your long-term objectives and ambitions. It's not too late to start making plans for the future. Before you make any modifications or improvements, you must first establish your objectives and ambitions. It's now or never to make great changes.

You're capable of a lot more than you give yourself credit for. One thing that prevents us from realizing our full potential is our own lack of self-confidence. Anyone can improve themselves and become a better person. That is the goal of development.

You are well on your way to being a better person once you begin to believe in yourself. There are several pathways to success. You can work as a singer, artist, writer, actor, dancer, or designer, among other things. The important thing to remember about growth is that it does not happen overnight. Changing your life and improving yourself requires time and effort.

One of the most common reasons people fail to achieve their objectives is a lack of clarity about what they want to accomplish and the measures necessary to get there. Here are seven easy strategies to help you tap into your untapped potential.

1. Make a list of what you desire: The first step is to jot down your future vision. What are your true desires in life? What is your motivation for wanting it? What would your life be like once you've reached your goal? Start thinking about how you can realize your vision once you've identified it.

2. Determine the actions you must take: After you've established your objective, you'll need to figure out how to get there. Start with the ultimate result if you aren't sure where to begin. What would you do if you succeeded in your goal? If you want to be a successful novelist, for example, you may start by writing a book. What would you do if you were to write this book? Would you require the services of a publisher? If that's the case, who would you approach? What would you have to do in order to get a publisher? If you're not sure where to begin, consider going backwards. Begin by considering the steps you'll need to take to reach your objective.

3. Write down the first step: Once you've determined the actions you'll need to take, write down the first one. It might be anything as simple as "create a book" or "research publishers."

4. Make a list of potential roadblocks: Once you've defined the actions you'll need to follow, consider any potential roadblocks to attaining your objective. For example, what are the things you'll need to do, for example, if you wish to lose weight? Consider where you could encounter difficulties and how you might overcome them. You should also consider whether you lack any talents or other resources that might aid you in achieving your objectives.

5. Determine the steps you'll take to overcome challenges: Write down the actions you'll need to overcome any difficulties after you've recognized them. Then go through your list of steps again to be sure you've covered everything. If you're not sure about something, talk to your adviser or a counselor about it.

6. Set a goal for each step: After you've written down the actions you'll need to take to reach your objective, be sure you set a goal for each one. If you want to publish a book, for example, you could set a target of writing 10 pages every day. This would be your initial step, and it may serve as a gauge for how far you've progressed. This aim might also be used as a yardstick for your progress.

7. Make a habit of doing something every day: If you're not sure where to begin, start by doing one small thing each day. If you want to write a book, for example, start by writing 10 pages every day. It's not difficult, and it'll help you stay motivated. Don't be concerned with what others are doing. You are the one person in charge of your life and choices. Don't worry about what other people think; do what feels right to you.

8. Make use of the "if/then" strategy: Using the "if/then" technique, you may develop a more effective plan. It assists you in identifying the particular measures you'll need to follow to achieve your objective. For example, consider the following: I'll write a book if I want to. Then I'll..

9. Consider the future: If you wish to do anything in the future, consider the steps that will be required. What are the measures you'll need to take? Make a list of your goals and then get started on implementing them.

10. Create a vision board: A vision board is a collection of images and words that represent your life goals. You may use this collage to remind yourself of your goals. What are your true desires in life? What is your motivation for wanting it? What would your life be like once you've reached your goal?

Everyone can realize their greatest potential and become the best they can be in this world. Your level of achievement is determined by your own hard work and efforts. We all have the potential to achieve greatness in our lives. Persistence is the key to success. You can do everything you set your mind to. All you have to do is pick a goal, work hard toward it, and stay the course.

We are all aware that time is valuable, and we should not waste it. There are numerous things we should do in life.

There are several tasks that are critical for us to complete. To achieve your life objectives, you must perform activities that are really beneficial to you.

It's time to wake up if you believe you can't accomplish some things because you don't know how to do them. It is entirely up to you what you do. We must abandon the notion that we are born with a preset set of traits and capabilities. Just because we are born with a certain skill or talent does not imply that we cannot develop it or modify it. You may enhance your life in a variety of ways. Taking lessons, attending courses, speaking with someone who has done it previously, or discovering methods to improve are some of these options. These things can assist you in improving your skills. You should not put off making adjustments until you believe there is no more room for improvement. It's time for you to realize your full potential.

You must first determine what you are capable of before you can determine what you can do. It's pointless to try to figure out what you can't accomplish since there's always something you can do. If you can accomplish anything, you can always discover a better way to do it. If you don't know how to do anything, you should learn it as soon as possible. You can locate free online lessons to learn how to accomplish stuff. You might also enlist the assistance of friends or family members. This will assist you in determining your capabilities. If you don't know how to do something, you must find a means to learn how to do it. If you have the ability to learn something new, you should try to learn everything there is to know about it. Make a plan to learn all you need to know. You can read articles or watch YouTube videos. You might also try taking lessons or talking to someone who has already done it.

Finally, keep in mind that anybody may become a great professional, but you won't be able to accomplish that level of excellence if you don't put in the work. You must be willing to put in the time and effort if you want to reach your full potential. There are no quick fixes when it comes to achieving your best self. So, what's preventing you from reaching your greatest potential?

Summary: *What if you could use psychology to tap into latent potential and live your greatest life? Understanding the psychology of human potential is the best approach to getting there. Knowing how to focus our thoughts is the key to success. According to studies, the average worker loses three hours each week owing to stress. Optimizing life is not about living on the edge or being terrified of happiness. It's all about choosing decisions that will lead to a life of plenty. If your to-do list is getting out of hand, it's time to take a step back and figure out what really has to be done right now. Make a list of your priorities to help you stay focused on the top three things that you know must be completed. People should always strive to improve their skills since they are capable of far more than they currently do. If you're feeling overwhelmed, delegate a tiny portion of your tasks to someone else.*

Even if you haven't found your calling yet, you should never give up giving it your all. Many people lack the guts to pursue their passions, but this does not mean they are failures. Optimizing your life and career means doing the things you should be doing but haven't been because of distractions and uninspiring chores. The world's most successful individuals don't suddenly decide to do what they do best one day. Stop doing things in the short term if you want to optimize your life and business.

This entails planning ahead of time what you're going to do and how you'll get there. Living and working is a mentality that focuses on long-term objectives rather than present necessities. Business people are constantly seeking the greatest strategy to ensure that their lives and enterprises are optimized. One thing that prevents us from realizing our full potential is our own lack of self-confidence. It's not too late to start making plans for the future and realize your potential.

One of the most common reasons people fail to achieve their objectives is a lack of clarity. Consider whether you lack any talents or other resources that might aid you in achieving your objectives. If you're unsure about something, talk to your adviser or counselor about it.

Don't worry about what other people think; do what feels right to you. Make a list of your goals and then get started on implementing them. Just because we are born with a certain skill or talent does not mean we cannot develop it or modify it. If you don't know how to do anything, you should learn it as soon as possible.

Chapter 3

Psychological Myths That Are Holding You Back From Your Dreams

Many of us have aspirations, ambitions, and objectives that we'd like to achieve. I'm not talking about the weird dreams and images you get after a few beers or a night of no sleep. I'm referring to your dreams. You had them when you were a kid, and you still have them now. I'm referring to the dreams that keep you up at night; you know the ones I'm referring to: dreams that make you happy, sad, or delighted. When we talk about dreams, we're talking about the things we desire in our lives. We all have goals, whether it's going to college, getting married, moving out of your parents' house, purchasing a house, or establishing a company. Dreams are the things we want to be able to achieve or possess. The difficulty is that many of us are unaware that we are trapped in our dreams.

We all have ambitions, but we all have constraints. We can't truly start moving forward with our ambitions unless we start analyzing our constraints. These limits have been dubbed "psychological misconceptions" by some. In this chapter, I'll go through some of the most common psychological fallacies that prevent you from achieving your goals. I'll explain why you're stifling your potential and how to overcome these psychological barriers.

Here are a few of the psychological myths that are preventing you from achieving your goals.

Psychological Myth #1: "I should just go with the flow if I'm not sure what I want to do." Life isn't always a straight line, as we all know. There are ups and downs, and many things we have no control over. We may, however, choose how we react to events. We have control over whether we have a favorable or negative reaction to anything. We must be flexible in our approach at times, but we must also be honest with ourselves. We're not really thinking about our objectives if we're continually questioning ourselves whether we should be doing anything; we're just responding to the situation. Because you're not actually thinking about it, you're just responding to the situation, you're having trouble making a decision. You don't have to be certain about what you want to accomplish with your life 100 percent of the time. All you have to do now is make an informed decision, and if you're still unsure, take a step back. There's no need to feel compelled to do something you're not sure about. Starting anything you're not sure about is not a good idea.

Psychological Myth #2: "Before I do something new, I need to be confident." We all suffer from a lack of self-assurance. Some of us are born with more self-assurance than others. However, I believe that many of us undervalue the importance of confidence in our ability to succeed. When we're in a scenario where we've had previous success, we may feel confident, but this isn't always the case. We can also be confident in situations where we are unfamiliar. The issue is that we often place much too much emphasis on self-assurance. We tend to overestimate how much confidence we need because we believe it is a magic medicine that will help us attain what we want in life. We believe that if we only had greater confidence, we would be able to do everything we set our minds to in life. While confidence can help you with some tasks, it won't be enough to help you achieve your objectives. You must be willing to put in a lot of effort and stick to your ideas. You must also be able to collaborate with others. In order to be successful in life, you will need to master a variety of skills. It will be tough for you to succeed if you don't know anything about anything, but that doesn't mean you should never attempt something new. You should, however, be able to confidently put yourself out there. If you're not confident, you're better off staying at home since you're not going to do anything. Instead, concentrate on the things that you can control: your confidence, your ability to learn new things, and your ability to improve your talents. This will help you become a better person and achieve your objectives.

Psychological Myth #3: "I have to be honest with myself." Being truthful with oneself is a crucial aspect of achieving success. Even if you believe you are correct, you must always be prepared to confess when you are incorrect. You'll never get far in life if you don't confess when you're wrong. If you want to be successful, you must be prepared to confess when you are mistaken. However, this does not imply that you must constantly be mistaken. Sometimes all you have to do is alter your viewpoint. Admitting when you're wrong isn't always easy, but you should always be willing to do so. This will assist you in becoming a better individual. You should also be willing to recognize when you are not ready for something; being honest with yourself is crucial. Acknowledging when you aren't ready for something will help you plan for the future. It's important to know what you want for the future, but it's even more important to recognize what you're not ready for. You should not be afraid to admit when you are unprepared for something. If you aren't prepared for anything, you must be honest with yourself about it. This will assist you in becoming a better individual.

Psychological Myth #4: "I can obtain what I want out of life if I work hard enough." In truth, it's more like this: "If I work hard enough, I'll figure out a way to escape having to work hard." "Work smarter, not harder" is a phrase we've all heard. On the surface, this statement appears easy and reasonable, but closer examination reveals that it is anything but. Most people fail to attain their life objectives because they spend too much time attempting to obtain what they desire rather than focusing on how to obtain what they require.

Psychological myth #5: "I need to be a particular age or have a specific amount of experience before I can start striving for the heavens,". If you don't learn from your errors, you'll never go anywhere. Anything may be learned as long as you know what you're doing. If you keep studying and trying, you can become an expert in everything you choose to learn.

Psychological Myth #6: "You're done for life if you fail once." This myth has been debunked several times. It's not true that if you fail once, you'll never succeed again. We learn from our errors, develop from them, and progress as a result of them. So, why do we keep making the same mistakes over and over again? What is it about failure that has such a bad connotation? So, why do we continue to fail? We are afraid of the negative emotions associated with failure because we are afraid of embarrassment, humiliation, shame, loss of face, rejection, being a fool, failure, being alone, being alone with ourselves, being alone with no one else, feeling powerless, being a loser, feeling stupid, feeling inferior, and being a disappointment. Failing is not always bad; it is not always embarrassing; it is not always a sign that we are weak or foolish; it is not always a sign that others will judge us negatively; it is not always a sign that we are being rejected; it is not always a sign that we are being rejected by others.Failure is an unavoidable component of achievement; it is the cost of trying. You move on when you fail, and you attempt something new when you succeed.

Psychological myth #7: "Everyone gets what they desire." This is, once again, untrue. Some of us are born with exceptional abilities and talent; others must work hard and exert effort to achieve our goals; and still others are fortunate enough to be born into a life that has been planned for us, allowing us to take advantage of opportunities and even live off the grid if we so desire. The fact is that there are several paths to achieving your goals in life; the trick is determining which one will lead you to your desired destination.

The concept of "impossible dreams" is a prevalent pitfall that prevents individuals from achieving their objectives. Many individuals believe that if they dream large, they will never achieve their goals because they lack the necessary willpower. Willpower, on the other hand, is not an all-powerful force. When we dream big but act little, our goals are no closer to being realized than if we hadn't dared to dream at all. So, let your dreams motivate you to rise from the dirt. I think that everyone has an impossible ambition that they wish to realize, whether it is as basic as getting into a prestigious college or as complex as founding a billion-dollar corporation. But the point is that we all have goals in life that we want to achieve.

The most common error people make while attempting to attain their objectives is believing that they are incapable of doing so. We all have hopes and dreams, and it's critical to keep them alive. We sometimes lose sight of our goals because we believe we have nothing to show for our efforts, or we believe that if we attempt, we will fail. But this isn't true; if we don't dream large, we'll never succeed. Dreaming big may be one of life's most powerful forces. When you think about it, there are two sorts of individuals in the world: those who dream big and those who dream tiny, and the latter will always triumph. So, why do you believe so many individuals claim, "I'm not capable of doing that?" Why do you think so many individuals believe they are incapable of achieving their goals? The explanation is that they believe they are incapable because they lack sufficient willpower. However, willpower is not an all-powerful force; it is a finite resource, and you can only control what you focus on.

Many people believe they are trapped and that there is no way to go forward. These individuals are mistaken; it is possible to achieve tremendous heights and great things in life. You must have objectives and know what you want to accomplish. These objectives might range from obtaining a higher position to beginning a new profession. If you do, you can succeed; all you have to do is believe in yourself and keep trying. If you work hard and never give up, you will succeed. Being the only one who believes in oneself is the most difficult thing to do. Others will lose faith in you if you don't trust yourself.

You must create and achieve goals in order to become a successful person. It's always better to learn from your errors than not to learn at all, no matter how many times you fail. The first stage is to figure out what you want to accomplish in life and create some objectives. Once you've done that, you'll need to figure out how to get things done. You can achieve this by enlisting the support of others or doing it alone. It depends on your circumstances. The first stage is to make a plan of action, which will include all of the actions you'll take to get there and will serve as your success blueprint. You must know the road to your destination as well as the difficulties you will encounter along the way. After you've created your strategy, you must continue to work on it every day. Make a list of all the elements of your strategy so you don't forget anything. Write down your objectives, and make sure you establish realistic goals for yourself. Always be positive and trust in yourself, but don't set your expectations too high. To be successful, you must have the appropriate attitude, a good approach to life, and confidence in yourself, as well as a love for what you do. If you do this, you will be able to achieve amazing things in your life. No matter how many times you fail, if you strive hard enough, you will succeed. You will not succeed if you do not put forth a strong effort. You must believe in yourself and strive to develop yourself every day by doing your best. To be successful, you must be willing to put in long hours and understand that each day will offer new problems and chances. It's critical to never give up and to constantly push oneself. You've got this. It is possible to achieve great things in life. Many individuals believe they are trapped, but they are incorrect; you can achieve amazing things.

You're not alone if you feel like you're caught in a rut. Because they accept psychological fallacies, most individuals are prevented from accomplishing their goals. It's all too easy to believe the myths, falsehoods, and justifications we tell ourselves to avoid taking action. These psychological roadblocks are preventing you from attaining your goals.

It's time to understand the truth about how you think and what you can do to overcome it if you want to attain your goals. You have a decision to make. You have the option of remaining stuck in your rut or breaking free and creating the life of your dreams.

What is psychological myopia, and how does it affect you?

Psychological myopia is a word used to describe a person's tendency to perceive only the difficulties that develop while dismissing all of the positive things that are going well when they are completely engrossed in an activity or undertaking. It's a cognitive bias that has to be recognized in order to be overcome. It has been reported in the news. When a newscaster misses an opportunity to emphasize a positive story in favor of highlighting a bad one, viewers grow irritated.

According to Harvard research, people in relationships who compare themselves to other people are more likely to develop psychological myopia. This is the same reason why we can't accept compliments: if you compare yourself to others, you'll constantly fall short and feel horrible about yourself. This is why being open-minded and keeping your eyes on the prize is a smart idea. Consider this: your objective isn't to impress everyone with your achievements. You're merely trying to make yourself happy and be satisfied with your achievements. "I need to get out more," "I need to do this," and "I need to lose weight" are common phrases.This is how we think: we see life as a series of chores and goals that must be completed in order for us to be happy, which is the polar opposite of pleasure. The fact is that the more work you put in, the less productive you are. Things will change the more you strive to alter them. What if you understood that you were the source of the problem? What if, instead of attempting to change others, you focused on transforming yourself? What if you discovered that the more you achieve, the less accomplished you are? What if, instead of attempting to change others, you focused on transforming yourself?

Taking credit for accomplishments might be a terrible idea from a psychological standpoint. Because you want to think you've accomplished something, you tend to focus primarily on the things you're doing well rather than the other tasks that remain unfinished. We focus on what we've done well instead of searching for methods to improve, and as a result, we overlook the areas where we may improve. Instead of declaring, "In the next month, I'm going to achieve x, y, and z," consider, "What may I improve on so that I can do these things more simply and efficiently in the future?" It will help you avoid falling into the trap of thinking you already know how to succeed.

How to overcome self-limiting negative thoughts that are preventing you from accomplishing your objectives.

Something in the way we talk to ourselves about ourselves is preventing us from achieving the goals we set for ourselves. We feel we know more than the rest of the world and that we aren't good enough to achieve our goals. In this book, I'll show you why you should quit believing in those restrictive and harmful attitudes. You've got this!

The notion that they are incapable of achieving their goals is a typical error made by people who fail to achieve their ambitions. This is frequently due to their belief that something is wrong with them or their situation. And, of course, if you don't believe you're capable of achieving anything, you'll never accomplish it. But that doesn't rule out the possibility of achieving your objectives. In fact, I've discovered that brilliant individuals tend to have a lot of self-limiting beliefs. This is because our experiences have an impact on what we believe about ourselves and our skills. When you've struggled with anything in the past, it's difficult to trust that you'll be able to accomplish it again. Because our brains are built to learn through experience, this is the case. The good news is that you can change your thinking and believe in your ability to attain your objectives.

It's all too easy to form negative self-limiting views about yourself and your skills, which function as impediments to success. To advance to the next level, you must break past these obstructions. It might feel like there are no options when you're mired in the muck of self-limiting ideas. It's difficult to think that you can break free from your shackles. However, the reality is that you can.

When you're not living up to your full potential, it's difficult to be your best. If you're anything like me, you're always looking for ways to improve. There are numerous areas in which I'd like to improve, whether it's my physique, my relationships, or my profession.

However, I've met a number of individuals who struggle to be their best in some aspects of their lives due to negative self-limiting ideas that prevent them from doing so. So, here are eight strategies to overcome these limiting ideas and become the best version of yourself and realize your ambitions.

1. Stop Trying to Be Someone Else: You don't have to fit in with the crowd. There's nothing wrong with being yourself. We all have something distinctive about us, yet we are also strikingly similar to one another. Everyone wants to be happy and accepted by their peers, family, and friends, as well as strangers.

2. Recognize Your Limiting Beliefs: One of the first steps is to recognize your limiting beliefs.What attitudes or beliefs are preventing you from being your best self? For example, perhaps you're not very good at relationships because you believe they're really difficult. Perhaps you aren't doing well at work because you believe you aren't clever enough. You can modify your limiting beliefs after you've identified them.

3. Change Your Words: Another technique for overcoming negative, self-limiting thoughts is to change your words.Try stating "I'm smart enough" instead of "I'm not smart enough" if you believe you aren't smart enough. If you feel that relationships are really difficult, try stating, "Relationships are simple."

4. Begin with a little change: Don't try to transform your entire life at once. Instead, begin with a single little modification and observe how things go. Perhaps you want to be more self-assured, so you tell yourself, "I'm going to be self-assured tomorrow."

5. *Keep At It:* Starting something new might be frightening, but if you keep at it and stick with it long enough, you'll succeed.

6. *Make A Vision Board:* Making a vision board is a great way to stay motivated.It assists you in visualizing your goals for the future. For your vision board, find a picture of the person or thing you wish to become. Next, make a list of the goals you wish to achieve.

7. *Change Your Surroundings:* Changing your surroundings is one way to change your environment.If you're having trouble with relationships, for example, you may alter your surroundings by relocating to a different section of town or obtaining a new roommate.

8. *Be More Positive:* We might get so wrapped up in the bad that we forget how much we can improve. If you're having a bad day, try one of these eight things for 30 days and see how you feel.

Finally, it's critical to remember that we can all be successful at something, and that in order to do so, we all require a plan. What do you hope to achieve? What are your plans for the next several months? To get there, what talents do you need to build and practice? Make a list of everything you'll need to get to your destination. Make a list of everything you believe you'll need to accomplish your objective. Then, when you're ready to give up, go through your list. This will give you a clear picture of what you're aiming for and make it easy to identify if you've been advancing in the wrong direction or not at all. You'll always be able to tell whether or not you're making progress if you keep track of your progress and what you're doing on a regular basis.

Summary: Many of us are unaware that we are trapped in our dreams. Dreams are the things we want to be able to achieve or possess. These limits have been dubbed "psychological misconceptions" by some. Many of us undervalue the importance of confidence in our ability to succeed. We tend to overestimate how much confidence we need because we believe it is a magic medicine that will help us attain what we want in life. Being truthful with oneself is a crucial aspect of achieving success. If you want to be successful, you must be prepared to admit when you are mistaken. Admitting when you're wrong isn't always easy, but you should always be willing to do so. Acknowledging when you aren't ready for something will help you plan for the future.

Some of us are born with exceptional abilities and talent; others must work hard and exert effort to achieve our goals. There are several paths to achieving your goals in life; the trick is determining which one leads you to your desired destination. Dreaming big may be one of life's most powerful forces. It is possible to achieve tremendous heights and great things in life.

You must have objectives and know what you want to accomplish. If you do, you can succeed; all you have to do is believe in yourself and keep trying. To be successful, you must have the appropriate attitude, a good approach to life, and confidence in yourself. You must believe in yourself and strive to develop yourself every day by doing your best. Each day will offer new problems and chances for you to try and succeed.

According to Harvard research, people who compare themselves to other people are more likely to develop psychological myopia. Being open-minded and keeping your eyes on the prize is a smart idea. Consider asking yourself, "What may I improve on so that I can do these things more simply and efficiently?". It's all too easy to form negative self-limiting views about yourself and your skills, which function as impediments to success. To advance to the next level, you must break past these obstructions.

Make a list of everything you believe you'll need to accomplish your objective. Then, when you're ready to give up, go through your list.

Chapter 4

Take Advantage of the Power Of Your Mind To Maximize Your Potentials

One of the greatest blessings that God has given to man is the ability to use your intellect to maximize your potential.

You've probably heard of hypnosis and self-hypnosis, but have you ever considered putting it to good use? It's true; we're all hypnotizable, and as we become older, we're more sensitive to suggestion manipulation. So, what's holding you back from taking advantage of this technology, and how can you make it work for you? Let's have a look.

A hypnotic state of mind is one in which a person may be convinced to do something they would not normally do if not for the hypnotist's suggestion. A hypnotized individual may recall events that occurred prior to undergoing hypnosis, but they are unable to do any tasks that involve motor skills or thinking abilities. They can also become very suggestible, giving their thoughts on subjects that are unrelated to the hypnotist and even obeying the hypnotist's directions despite knowing that they are lying to themselves. Hypnosis is most effective when used as a treatment because it allows you to make your subconscious mind open to ideas while in a hypnotic state. Your conscious mind will no longer interfere with the recommendations after they have been made. This strategy may be used to boost your self-esteem, lose weight, conquer anxieties, build endurance, and acquire new abilities.

Your mind's ability to modify your life is boundless. If you genuinely want to learn something and are prepared to put in the work, you can learn whatever you set your mind to. In truth, the majority of individuals are unwilling to put in the effort. When they don't want to accomplish anything, they make up a few excuses for themselves.

The notion is that you may better your life by maximizing your potential by harnessing the power of your thoughts. You are born with a certain amount of potential, and it is up to you to learn how to maximize it. Visualization, self-hypnosis, meditation, and other similar techniques can help you achieve this. As a consequence, you'll be able to realize your full potential and be happier than you've ever been. How can you harness your mind's power? When you get an idea, think about it and attempt to picture it in your mind's eye. Imagine yourself in the future and how things will be different from how they are today.

Learn to picture yourself as the person you desire. Consider what life would be like if you had the ideal career, a lovely home, and a loving family. Consider your positive qualities and imagine yourself living in an ideal environment. What kind of world would this be? You may imagine yourself living in this ideal environment and feeling the happiness, the energy flowing through your body, and the tranquility that you would experience. This is how you can reach your full potential. Simply visualize what you want to happen in your life, and you will achieve it.

Discover the fundamentals of self-hypnosis. Self-hypnosis is a method for teaching oneself to hypnotize oneself. Hypnosis works by raising your awareness of how your body operates, allowing you to more quickly learn how to regulate it. You will be able to do things that you previously believed were impossible, and you will be able to accomplish your objectives. Visualization can help you achieve your objectives.

Find out how to meditate. If you want to learn to meditate, you must first learn to empty your mind of any bad ideas and concentrate on good ones. Imagining a pleasant environment in your mind is the best way to begin meditating. You must see yourself at this wonderful location and feel the tranquility and happiness that you would experience there. After that, you must see yourself in the ideal world and you must envision yourself living in this ideal environment. You will be able to feel the serenity, happiness, and love that you would feel in this world as you continue to meditate.

It's difficult to dispute the power of a cheerful mindset. You must focus on acquiring the ability to be optimistic if you want to be a top performer. We all have a natural predisposition to be gloomy and negative; our mood, the events around us, and the opinions we have about ourselves and others all impact us. However, if you can cultivate a more optimistic attitude, you will be able to improve the quality of your life. It is the most effective treatment for anxiety and despair, as well as the most effective means of overcoming procrastination and achieving more.

According to research published in the Journal of Clinical Psychology, people who are sad make decisions based on pessimism, whereas those who are positive make decisions based on optimism. When you keep a positive attitude, you make better judgments because you base them on facts rather than emotions. To put it another way, optimism enables you to make judgments based on facts rather than emotions.

It will assist you in being more efficient in your daily life. In my opinion, the largest barrier to becoming optimistic is our natural propensity to dwell on the unpleasant aspects of life. On a daily basis, we are inundated with unpleasant news and information. Every terrible occurrence that occurs is covered by news sources all around the world. This makes us feel horrible about ourselves and gives us the impression that we are in worse shape than we are. However, if we take a step back and consider the broader picture, we might discover that we are in a far better situation than we may believe. If you were born into a wealthy household, for example, you are unlikely to be homeless. You're not going to go hungry. You have food, housing, clothing, a warm bed, an excellent education, and a plethora of other advantages. The same may be said for many other aspects of life. We have a tendency to focus on what we lack. We should instead concentrate on what we do have. We are considerably more fortunate than we think. The following activity can assist you in developing a positive attitude:

- Make a list of one thing you don't want to happen. Anything might be the case. It's possible that you don't want to be late for work, or that you don't want to make a mistake. It's possible that you don't want to make a blunder in front of a friend or loved one. Simply choose something that is meaningful to you.

- After that, think about one thing you do want to happen.Anything might be the case. It's possible that you want to be on time for work, make a good first impression on your boss, or spend quality time with your friends and family.

- Finally, take a step back and consider all of the positive aspects of your life. You may believe that you are in a bad situation because you are unemployed and unable to find work, but you actually have a lot to be thankful for. You have food to eat, clothes to wear, a comfortable bed to sleep in, an education to help you learn new things, a warm house to live in, and many more things for which you should be grateful.

You are what you think you are, "is a phrase I'm sure we've all heard. This means that we all have the ability to compel ourselves to act in specific ways. There is always the possibility of change, no matter what we do. We are exactly who we believe we are. We must consider our lives in a favorable light. We cannot improve ourselves if we believe we are doing anything wrong or that we have no future. In reality, we will constantly be depressed if we adopt a pessimistic mentality. This makes us feel like a failure, which can lead to a pessimistic outlook on life. We will be dissatisfied if we believe we can not do anything. This might lead to negative ideas like, "Why even try?" It is certain that you will fail if you believe you will. If you believe you are good, you will get better. You will feel depressed if you believe you are a loser. You will have bad feelings if you have negative thoughts. When we think positively, we feel better, and when we feel better, we think positively.

We must all learn to regulate our emotions and strike the proper balance between being positive and negative. It's vital to remember that when things are going well, it's quite easy to be joyful. When things aren't going well, though, it's more difficult to be cheerful. We all have to deal with adversity from time to time; you can't constantly be cheerful. Sometimes we have no choice but to confront the truth. We can't always do what we want; we have to keep a realistic perspective on life; and we can't always get what we want.Life isn't always kind.

We are exactly who we think we are. All that we are emerges from our ideas, and we create the world with our thoughts. We become what we think. As a result, anything we discover about ourselves may be used to alter our thoughts and feelings. To put it another way, you create what you think about!

Ways to Harness the Power of Your Mind to Achieve Your Goals

It's not about how much money you make, where you live, or what sort of automobile you drive; it's about the power of your mind. It all comes down to how strong your mind is and how much you can do with it. No one else will believe in you if you don't believe in yourself. Your mentality determines your capacity to do almost anything you set out to do.

We all have advantages and disadvantages. It is critical to exploit our strengths and improve our flaws if we want to be the greatest. You must learn to maximize your potential, which you may do by employing your intellect. We are all talented in different ways, and no one is perfect in every way. If you utilize your thoughts to aid you, you can achieve your full potential. You should strive to think positively and consider how you might make things better.

103

Put your best foot forward at all times. Don't be concerned if you are unhappy; instead, make an effort to do things that will make you happy. You must make good choices if you want to make good ones.It is all up to you, so do whatever it takes to improve yourself and achieve your goals. You have the power to change things in your life for the better.

The most successful individuals aren't looking for easy ways to get ahead. Instead, they figure out how to tap into the mindpower that we all have. There are various methods to unlock the power of our mind to bring us anything we desire, whether it's tapping into our intuition, accessing the subconscious, or developing a powerful attitude.

We are all one-of-a-kind as people. We each have our own set of skills and personalities. We also have distinct ways of thinking, setting objectives, and caring for ourselves.

To be successful, you must be able to notice people's differences and find a way to work around them. It's critical to have the appropriate attitude and approach to things if you want to be successful. There are a plethora of factors that go into achieving success. The first step is to have a better understanding of oneself. You will have a better grasp of the world and be able to make modifications to match your requirements once you are aware of your strengths and shortcomings. It is critical to understand how to overcome your flaws as well as how to deal with failures in order to deal with disappointments. It's critical to be realistic about your objectives and adaptable when things don't go according to plan. Your strategy should be adjustable and flexible.

Let's look at the top five most powerful attitudes and how to use them to attain life success.

1. A Champion's Attitude: A champion's attitude is one that is driven by ambition, excitement, and optimism. Champions don't let their circumstances define who they are or what they believe. They are confident in their capacity to achieve, regardless of the circumstances. They have an optimistic attitude towards life and seize any opportunity that comes their way. A champion thinks that the universe is on their side and that they will keep going even when things become rough. When you're in a horrible position, it's tempting to allow your ideas and actions to be dictated by the circumstances. You may lose faith in your capacity to overcome challenges. This is when you need to remember to think like a champion.

2. Visionary Mentality: A visionary mentality is one that is driven by passion and belief. The concept of something larger than themselves inspires visionaries. They have great dreams and a fresh view of the world. They don't simply see the world through rose-colored glasses; they perceive it as if it were a completely different universe. Visionaries recognize that success is an experience rather than a destination. It's not about how much money they make, but rather how much effect they can have on the world. Being a visionary is difficult. You must be willing to take risks and go against the grain. To believe in yourself and your ideas requires the guts to do so. It doesn't matter if you aren't a visionary yourself; you can still help others become visionaries.

3. The Master's Attitude: The master's attitude is fuelled by discipline, dedication, and knowledge. Master craftspeople are continually seeking ways to improve. They are the ones that understand that unless they are ready to always learn, they will not grow. They recognize that you can never stop learning, and they are constantly on the lookout for new approaches to attain their objectives. They are motivated by passion as well as a strong sense of purpose. They recognize that in order to achieve anything great, you must be willing to take chances and that nothing great comes easily. Being a master implies that you're always learning and attempting to improve your existing situation. You understand that every day is an opportunity to learn something new, and you refuse to allow your past failures to stop you from achieving your goals. It takes some time to get there, but the payoff is definitely worth the effort.

4. The Entrepreneur's Attitude: The entrepreneur's attitude is one of tenacity, perseverance, and optimism. Entrepreneurs are motivated by the urge to create something new. They are always looking for new methods to bring a concept to life. They're always searching for new methods to improve their company's efficiency, and they're always on the lookout for new chances to help them expand. Being an entrepreneur entails taking chances, being adaptable, and embracing change. It is not for the faint of heart; it is a call to those who are dedicated to excellence.

5. The Investor's Attitude: The investor's attitude is driven by enthusiasm, devotion, and trust. The ambition to develop long-term wealth drives investors. An investor will go to whatever lengths to achieve his or her financial objectives, regardless of the problems, impediments, or repercussions that may arise. The investor's attitude will not only lead to investment success, but it will also affect their activities as investors. As an investor, you must be ready for anything.

11 Characteristics of Highly Successful Individuals

What are successful people's habits? What are some of the things they do on a daily basis to ensure their success?

Successful individuals are all around you, if you think about it. Your parents, teachers, friends, and acquaintances are among them. They are those who have excelled in their chosen industries or professions. What distinguishes them is their ability to succeed in the face of adversity.

Many of these folks had no advantages in life and were frequently born into low-income or low-social-status homes. Recently, I've been reading a lot about how people might attain success and happiness in their lives. I've discovered that successful people have specific routines that assist them in attaining success while also keeping them happy. Here are 11 behaviors that successful individuals have in common that you might adopt to improve your life:

• *They have a grateful attitude:* Most successful people appear to be grateful for what they have.They are grateful for what they have and the chances that have been provided to them. They also recognize the value of what they have and are eager to share it with others. You are more likely to succeed in life if you feel good about yourself.

• *They Practice Self-Discipline:* Successful people are self-disciplined, and they do not allow a lack of discipline to hold them back. They accept responsibility for their actions and are open to making adjustments when necessary. They are prepared to put in the effort necessary to attain their objectives.

• *They Have a Positive Attitude:* People who are successful have a positive outlook on life. They don't let bad ideas or emotions get in the way of their success. They are focused on their goals and recognize that they will need to put in a lot of effort to succeed.

• ***They Have a Clear Vision:*** Most successful people have a clear vision.They know what they want out of life and are prepared to work hard to achieve it. They can see the final objective and are prepared to put in the effort to achieve it. They know where they're headed, but they also realize how far they have to go.

• ***They Have An Open Mind:*** Successful people keep an open mind.They are open to new information and eager to adjust their minds. They are aware, however, that they are correct in some areas and incorrect in others. People that are successful do not get mired down in their own thoughts. They recognize that others have their own points of view and that they cannot force others to agree with theirs.One of the reasons why successful individuals are so easy to work with is because of this.

• ***They are self-motivated:*** The majority of successful people are self-motivated.They are prepared to put in the effort and sacrifice necessary to attain their objectives. This is the distinction between successful and unsuccessful individuals. The issue is that most of us are unwilling to go to great lengths to attain our objectives. We are unwilling to make sacrifices, lack the necessary attitude, or just refuse to put in the effort.

• *They Have Solid Interpersonal Relationships:* Successful people have solid interpersonal relationships.They understand that they can rely on others to assist them and that they can rely on them for assistance. They are willing to put in the effort to form a bond with someone.

• *They Are Willing to Seek Help:* Successful people are not afraid to ask for help when they need it.They are willing to put in the effort in order to receive assistance from others. They understand they won't be able to complete the task on their own. Successful people recognize that they will never be able to achieve their goals without the help of others. They understand that success is the result of a mix of hard work, enthusiasm, and collaboration. It takes courage to ask for help.

• ***They Are Not Afraid to Take Risks:*** Successful people are not afraid to take risks.They don't let their fear of failure keep them from taking chances. They are willing to take risks and attempt new things, and they are prepared to fail in order to succeed.

• ***They Are Willing to Learn New Things:*** Successful people are eager to learn new things.They are prepared to take chances and experiment with new ideas. They understand that in order to be successful, they will need to master new skills. They understand that the road to success is not always a straight one, and that learning from errors and achievements is a necessary part of the process. In truth, every individual's significant accomplishment can only be reached via continuous learning. This implies that education is a necessary component of life.

• ***They Take Responsibility for Their Actions:*** Successful people take responsibility for their actions.They understand that they are in charge of their own success and that they must be prepared to adapt when necessary. The good news is that you have the ability to transform your life if you are prepared to accept full responsibility for your choices. You'll be able to live the life you want as well. You are not relinquishing your authority when you accept responsibility for your actions.

Finally, a person is nothing more than a collection of habits and viewpoints. A habit is a refined and streamlined mental process that has evolved into a new mental process. You may help your brain operate at its best by improving and simplifying existing processes. As long as you are willing to put in the effort, you can optimize the efficiency and power of your brain for the rest of your life. Changing one's beliefs and actions can be a lifetime process for some people. You must master the mental tools you will need throughout your life to speed your progress.

***Summary:** Learn to picture yourself as the person you desire. Imagining a pleasant environment in your mind is the best way to begin meditating. People who are sad make decisions based on pessimism, whereas those who are positive make decisions based on optimism.*

When you keep a positive attitude, you make better judgments because you base them on facts rather than emotions. Optimism enables you to be more efficient in your daily life. Take a step back and consider all of the positive aspects of your life. We are considerably more fortunate than we think. We are exactly who we think we are.

We must consider our lives in a favorable light. We cannot improve ourselves if we believe we are doing anything wrong or that we have no future. When we think positively, we feel better and are more likely to achieve our goals. The most successful individuals aren't looking for easy ways to get ahead. They figure out how to tap into the mindpower that we all have.

To be successful, you must be able to notice people's differences and find a way to work around them. You must make good choices if you want to make good ones. It's crucial to be realistic about your objectives and adaptable when things don't go according to plan. Being a visionary is difficult; you must be willing to take risks and go against the grain. Master craftspeople are continually

117

seeking ways to improve, and are constantly on the lookout for new approaches.

The entrepreneur's mindset is one of tenacity, perseverance, and optimism. Entrepreneurs are motivated by the urge to create something new. Investors' mindset is driven by enthusiasm, devotion, and trust. Successful individuals have specific routines that assist them in attaining success while keeping them happy. People who are successful have a positive outlook on life.

Successful people are self-disciplined, and they do not allow a lack of discipline to hold them back. They are prepared to put in the effort necessary to attain their objectives. People that are successful do not get mired down in their own thoughts. Successful people are not afraid to ask for help when they need it. They understand that success is the result of hard work, enthusiasm, and collaboration.

They are willing to take risks and attempt new things, and they are prepared to fail in order to succeed. Every individual's significant accomplishment can only be reached via continuous learning. A person is nothing more than a collection of habits and viewpoints.

Chapter 5

What is the ONE Thing That Will Make You Succeed? (The Ultimate Secret)

I've read about some of today's best entrepreneurs who make millions of dollars each year, and what impresses me the most is that they all have one thing in common: they are fixated on one thing.

It's the thing that keeps them up at night. It's the only thing that motivates them to get out of bed every day. It's the one thing they can't leave the house without doing.

Now it's up to you to decide what your "one thing" is.

It's possible that the question is a little trickier than it appears. What if you have no idea what your ONE THING is? What if you have no idea where to begin? So, in this chapter, we'll look at this one thing in greater detail and get further into the notion. But first, let's talk about how you can start generating more money, becoming more successful, and living the life of your dreams.

1. Begin with your passion: The first step to producing more money is to ask yourself, "What do I care about?" One of the most crucial questions you'll ever ask yourself is this one. If you can figure out what you are actually passionate about, you'll be able to establish a life for yourself that is centered on something that makes you happy and content. If you don't know what your passion is, you should ponder it for a while. If you do discover your passion, you'll need to delve deep to figure out exactly what it is you're enthusiastic about. Art, athletics, and technology are all possibilities. Don't just assume you know what you're passionate about because you're sitting there. Ask yourself specific questions about your passions and what you feel like you might get enthusiastic about on a daily basis.

2. Create A Vision For Your Life: The second stage of getting more money is to create a vision for your life. You may now use this information to develop a vision for yourself after you know what you're passionate about. To put it another way, you must visualize what your life would be like if you were living your ideal life. It's critical that you have a clear mental image of what this life looks like; if you can't see yourself clearly in your vision, you'll never achieve this level of accomplishment. So, what are your options? To begin, you must first ask yourself, "What do I want my life to look like?" Then you'll need to put down what you believe is possible for you to achieve. Then you'll need to consider how you'll get there. This entails considering all of the measures you'll need to take to get there. For example, you can consider the measures necessary to obtain a new job, obtain a promotion, save money, and so on. This will assist you in developing a future vision. You will be able to become enthused about this vision and keep your motivation strong if you can clearly see yourself in it.

3. *Create Objectives:* The next stage is to set objectives. Now, when I say "establish goals," I don't mean that you should just put down some arbitrary, generic objectives that you have no intention of achieving. I'm talking about setting concrete, quantifiable, and attainable goals. It's also critical that you create objectives that are difficult but not impossible to achieve. After you've determined your objectives, you'll need to put them into action. This means you'll have to do things like: start working on your objectives every day; make a strategy to achieve your goals; and write them down every day.

4. *Don't Give Up:* If you want to achieve anything in life, you must stay motivated. So, after you've defined your objectives, it's critical that you stick to them. You must ensure that you remain devoted to them and that nothing stands in your way of completing them. In reality, one of the main reasons why most individuals fail to achieve their objectives is that they give up too soon. When things get tough, they quit working hard and give up on their aspirations. However, if you work hard and remain devoted, you will be able to achieve more than most others who have never put forth any effort toward their goals.

5. *Have a Plan B:* The fifth and last stage is to have a backup plan. There will be no issues if you complete everything precisely. However, if something goes wrong or you make a mistake, you'll need a backup plan. You'll need a strategy for getting back on track and avoiding a major setback. For example, if you've been trying to lose weight for months and eventually shed five pounds, you could start to feel a lot better about yourself. However, if your diet begins to fail and you gain five pounds, you will feel awful about yourself. That is why having a backup plan is crucial. Keeping a diet notebook can help you keep track of your progress and stay focused.You may also use it to keep track of the various foods you're eating. After you've written down everything you eat, you'll be able to determine how many calories you consume each day. By doing so, you'll be able to see how well you're doing on your diet. To prevent getting disappointed, always have a back-up plan.

You can only succeed if you focus on one subject. It takes a lot of effort and discipline. If you want to be successful, you must work hard every day and stay motivated in order to achieve your objectives. People that put in a lot of time and effort into life are the ones who achieve. They are not frightened of failure or rejection by others, and they do not readily become disheartened. They feel that they can do everything they set their minds to. If you want to make a difference in your life, you must think positively and stay motivated to achieve it. If you stay focused and committed to your aims, you can achieve your objectives. People that are successful work hard to achieve their objectives, do not give up easily, and are aware that there may be setbacks along the way. They, on the other hand, continue to work hard and achieve their goals. In order to stay motivated and productive, you must learn to regulate your emotions.

How to Find Your One Thing and Make It Big

Do you have a dream that has been bothering you for a long time? Do you wish there was a way to make it happen but don't know where to start? Have you ever felt like you're searching in circles for your "one thing?" Maybe someone urged you to start with one item and see what occurs, but you're not sure where to start. Or perhaps you've considered numerous options and aren't sure which is the best fit for you. Perhaps you're in a rut. You're getting worried about what you're going to do next. Perhaps you believe you're losing out on important chances. The fact is that finding the one item that will have a significant impact on your life can be really difficult. However, all you need to do is be enthusiastic about one subject and make the most of it.

You have a lot on your plate, and you need to figure out how to get everything done. This can be problematic since some of your initiatives are critical while others are not. When you're doing too many things, though, it's easy to become confused. This is a serious issue since you may end up doing nothing. You can have a lot of things, but if you don't do anything, nothing will get done. Even if you can't accomplish everything you desire, you should find a way to do one thing very well. You must have a vision and set personal objectives. You will find a way to accomplish them if you do so. You need to be well organized. That is why it is critical to organize your initiatives. You must ensure that you have the necessary resources and that you have sufficient time to accomplish the project. You should also create goals for yourself. You must ensure that you keep on top of your game in order to do more in a day. You will undoubtedly become overwhelmed if you attempt to accomplish too much.

There's something remarkable about being devoted to a single cause. We've all heard that having several skills is advantageous. Isn't it true that you should aim to master more than one? When you're just starting out, that's fantastic advice, but you don't want to stretch yourself too thin. You'll feel overwhelmed if you try to tackle too many things at once, which is the last thing you need when starting a new endeavor. You may have the energy and enthusiasm to accomplish a lot of things when you first start your business, but it won't take long for you to burn out, and if you burn out, you'll have to put in a lot of effort to get your business back on track. Instead, concentrate on one item, one passion, or one concept. It makes no difference whether the thing is physical or mental. For example, because writing is my one passion, I spend the majority of my time creating novels. You could, however, be enthusiastic about a different sort of endeavor. Find that one activity that fires you up inside, whether it's cooking, basketball, vehicle repair, or sewing clothing. Whatever it is, focus on it. Here are some of the benefits of having a strong interest in something:

• *You'll Develop a Better Self-Awareness:* When you're enthusiastic about something, you're more inclined to do it for the right reasons. You'll want to learn more about your passion because you'll want to understand why it's so essential to you. This is true whether your love is writing, cooking, or something else. It assists you in gaining a better knowledge of yourself as well as assists you in being more successful in your business. You'll discover things about yourself that will benefit you in your career and in life, such as how to deal with pressure, criticism, and rejection.

• *You'll Be More In Touch With What Really Matters:* When you're enthusiastic about something, you'll start to pay attention to the details. If you're enthusiastic about writing, for example, you'll begin to notice things that have a greater impact on your writing and business than anything else. That's because you'll only devote your time and attention to things that are important to you. When you're enthusiastic about writing, you'll notice more things linked to it, which will help you grasp what works and what doesn't.

• *You'll Develop More Relationships:* If you're passionate about something, you'll want to connect with others who share your passion. This is especially true when you're just getting your business off the ground. You'll want to surround yourself with like-minded individuals who can assist you in learning, providing guidance, and informing you of what you need to know. When you're enthusiastic about anything, you'll start to notice people who are as well, and you'll want to hang out with them. You'll be able to learn from them as they become your friends, mentors, and coworkers.

• *You'll have a good time because passion is enjoyable:* Being enthusiastic about something makes you joyful. It makes you feel wonderful and encourages you to continue doing it. You'll want to write more if you're enthusiastic about writing, and you'll want to cook more if you're passionate about cooking. When you're doing something you enjoy, your energy levels will rise, and you'll feel more like yourself.

You could find your "one thing" if you want to get rich rapidly and retire early. You'll also need "one thing" if you want to establish a business and make it a huge success.

"One thing" is something you can do exceptionally well and that generates a lot of money for you in a short length of time. As a result of this increased income, you will be able to work less and spend more time with your family and friends.

"One thing" isn't just a pastime or something you do on the weekends or when you're bored. It's a manner of thinking, doing, and living that's laser-focused.

It's possible that you won't be able to do "one thing" right away. In reality, creating just one item may take years. You may need to work in a variety of sectors, gain new skills, and seek out mentors. However, you will ultimately find that one thing that will lead to great things.

Have you ever seen anything so great that you kept thinking about it every day and even made it a part of your routine? It's been stated that when individuals are motivated, it's usually by something or someone. If you're

132

inspired by animals, for example, you probably appreciate seeing them in their natural environment, in a zoo, or even on a billboard. You may enjoy paintings, sculptures, or pictures of prominent artists and/or their work if you are motivated by art. The list could go on and on. The point is that when we are inspired by something or someone, it is typically the case that this object or person has had an impact on our lives in some way, shape, or form, and inspiration can be transitory when it comes to writing or any other sort of creative activity. When it does happen, though, it may be genuinely life-changing and lead to amazing achievement.

There's a lot of discussion about discovering your passion and calling, but one of the most significant lessons learned from the storytellers on this list is how to make your dream a reality. It doesn't always go according to plan, but that's part of the fun. However, there are occasions when you discover that what you thought was your thing isn't.

133

Or that you lack the necessary talent or desire to pursue it, and once those facts are discovered, the next stage is to choose what you will do next. This might be frightening, but it can also be freeing. You may focus your efforts on what you're excellent at and what you want to do after you know what you're good at and what you're not.

Finding your one thing might be difficult. You must test a variety of options before deciding on the best one for you. When you attempt different things, you'll discover what your one thing is. You should try a variety of things to find what suits you best. You may enjoy certain things while hating others. If that's the case, it's time to make a change.

Keeping a journal is one approach to finding your one thing. Writing down what you do and how you feel after each activity allows you to keep track of what you do and how you feel after each activity.This will assist you in determining which activities make you happiest. You may also utilize the material in your diary to discover your strengths and weaknesses, as well as what makes you sad. You'll be able to figure out what you like to do if you write down what you enjoy and don't like to do. A personality test might help you figure out what you enjoy doing. You may determine which activities to incorporate into your lifestyle once you've discovered what you're excellent at and what you don't want to do. What you put into your lifestyle is what you will get out of it. You should choose the activities that you wish to incorporate into your daily routine.

17 Ways That One Thing Will Help You Achieve Your Goals

Here are 17 different ways your ONE thing might help you thrive in life. But keep in mind that even if you can't accomplish everything at once, you can always start with one.

135

1. Focus on one thing you can do right now to improve your chances of success.

2. Set a small but effective goal for yourself.

3. Choose one activity that will help you achieve your objective.

4. One tiny step at a time, write down what you know about your aim.

5. Break the objective down into smaller chunks.

6. Pretend you're an aspiring athlete going to compete in a race.

7. Visualize yourself succeeding and reaching your goal.

8. Create a plan for achieving your goal.

9. Don't set the bar too high for yourself.

10. Make use of your imagination.

11. Keep in mind that the more you do, the more you will achieve.

12. If you don't achieve your objective immediately, don't become disheartened.

13. Seek feedback and become comfortable with criticism.

14. Always question yourself, "Why?"

15. If you hit a wall, push yourself even harder.

16. Make a daily effort to make progress toward your objective.

17. Never, ever give up.

Finally, you must define concrete, quantifiable, achievable, reasonable, and time-bound goals. You will set yourself up for success if you follow this model. The secret to success is to ask oneself one question all the time: "What's next?" There will be several occasions when you will wonder, "What's next?" Make it your own obligation to put yourself in the best possible position for success by prioritizing your future self. Examine if the goals you've previously established are putting you on the path to success. You can make better judgments and prepare for success in all facets of your life when you know what's coming next. You will lose out on a lot if you don't ask yourself, "What's next?" You will miss out on a lot if you don't ask yourself, "What's next?"

Summary: What is the ONE Thing That Will Make You Succeed? (The Ultimate Secret) is a series of questions and answers on how to generate more money and live the life of your dreams. If you want to achieve anything in life, you must first establish goals. It's critical that you create objectives that are difficult but not impossible to achieve.

If something goes wrong or you make a mistake, you'll need a backup plan for getting back on track. People that put in a lot of time and effort into life are the ones who achieve. If you want to make a difference in your life, you must think positively and stay motivated. Finding the one thing that will have a significant impact on your life can be really difficult.

All you need to do is be enthusiastic about one subject and make the most of it. You must ensure that you keep on top of your game in order to do more in a day. Being enthusiastic about something makes you joyful and encourages you to continue doing it. When you're passionate about something, you'll want to connect with others who share your passion.

"One thing" is something you can do exceptionally well that generates a lot of money in a short amount of time. It's possible that you won't be able to do "one thing" right

away. However, you will ultimately find that one thing that will lead to great things. You may enjoy certain things while hating others. If that's the case, it's time to make a change. Writing down what you do and how you feel after each activity will help you determine which activities make you happiest. The secret to success is to ask oneself one question all the time: "What's next?".

Gratitude

I'd want to express my gratitude for taking the time to read this book; I hope you enjoyed it and found it informative. I'd welcome your feedback regardless of whether I succeeded or not, because I put a lot of effort into making this book incredibly valuable and powerful for everyone in my audience and readers.

Please let me know what you think; I'm curious to hear how this book has benefited you. I'd be grateful if you could leave a review on the product's retail page stating how this book has helped you. Nothing makes me happier than knowing that my work has helped someone achieve their goals and advance in life; it also motivates me to continue improving so that I can better serve you. Your opinion is quite valuable to me.

Go to the product's retail page to share your success story.

If your feedback is negative, it's possible that you weren't impressed enough, or that you have a suggestion, inaccuracy, or criticism that needs to be addressed; we apologize for the inconvenience (remember, we are human, we are not perfect, and we are constantly striving to improve).

Please send your feedback, suggestion, or complaint to "adebayofolusho2017@gmail.com" rather than posting it on the book's retail page so that required edits, improvements, and implementation may be done quickly

for a better reading experience.

Once again, thank you for taking the time to read this

book.

Acknowledgements

All credit belongs to God. I'd also want to thank my wonderful family, partner, fans, readers, friends, and customers for their constant support and words of encouragement.

About The Author

Adebayo F. Dorcas is a life coach and nutritionist who wrote "Maximizing Your Potential," a book about habits, decision-making, and the attainment of goals.

For many years, millions around the world have benefited from Adebayo F. Dorcas' health and personal development coachings, which have led the world in creating and launching massive incentive prizes to promote radical innovations for the benefit of humanity.

Her approach to her discipline is more integrated and functional. Her main goal is to help people figure out what they want to do and become the person they want to be in different fields, so that they can build a healthy, well-rounded lifestyle that fits their needs and allows them to perform at their best.

Lightning Source UK Ltd.
Milton Keynes UK
UKHW012055100123
415145UK00002B/29